KIDS CAN COPE

Step Back from Frustration

by Gill Hasson

illustrated by Sarah Jennings

free spirit
PUBLISHING®

Published in North America by Free Spirit Publishing Inc., Minneapolis, Minnesota, 2021

Library of Congress Cataloging-in-Publication Data
Names: Hasson, Gill, author. | Jennings, Sarah, illustrator.
Title: Step back from frustration / by Gill Hasson ; illustrated by Sarah Jennings.
Description: Minneapolis : Free Spirit Publishing Inc., 2021. | Series: Kids can cope | Audience: Ages 6–9
Identifiers: LCCN 2020025919 | ISBN 9781631986161 (hardcover)
Subjects: LCSH: Frustration—Juvenile literature. | Emotions—Juvenile literature.
Classification: LCC BF575.F7 H37 2021 | DDC 155.4/1247—dc23
LC record available at https://lccn.loc.gov/2020025919

Reading Level Grade 3; Interest Level Ages 6–9;
Fountas & Pinnell Guided Reading Level N

Edited by Alison Behnke and Marjorie Lisovskis

10 9 8 7 6 5 4 3 2 1
Printed in China
H137701020

Free Spirit Publishing Inc.
6325 Sandburg Road, Suite 100
Minneapolis, MN 55427-3674
(612) 338-2068
help4kids@freespirit.com
freespirit.com

First published in 2021 by Franklin Watts, a division of Hachette Children's Books · London, UK, and Sydney, Australia

Copyright © The Watts Publishing Group, 2021

The rights of Gill Hasson to be identified as the author and Sarah Jennings as the illustrator of this Work have been asserted in accordance with the Copyright, Designs and Patents Act, 1988.

Series editor: Jackie Hamley

Series designer: Cathryn Gilbert

Step Back from Frustration

by Gill Hasson

illustrated by Sarah Jennings

What is frustration?

Frustration happens when you can't do something
or can't have something you want.
You may feel frustrated when you have to wait,
when you don't understand, when someone doesn't listen
to you, or when you keep trying to do something
but can't quite make it work.

You might get frustrated when things don't happen the way you expected them to. Or when you can't find or reach something you're looking for.

It's like you're on the right road to where you want to go, but things are blocking the way. You get close—maybe you can see where you want to be—but you just can't get there.

How do you feel when you're frustrated?

When you're frustrated you might feel like you are getting more and more wound up or angry. You may feel tense and hot. You might grit your teeth and clench your fists.

Frustration can also lead to feeling helpless.
You might get discouraged and feel stuck,
like it's not worth trying anymore.

What do you do?

When you feel frustrated, do you jump up and down? Do you shout and scream? Slam things or throw them around?

AAARRGGHH!

Maybe you get so wound up that you end up damaging the thing you were trying to make or do.

Or do you bottle it all up but feel like you're boiling inside?

Perhaps you get upset and start to cry. You might stop trying to do something and just give up.

The wheel of frustration

Frustration can feel like being on a wheel that spins around and around. As it spins, you get more and more angry or discouraged, and the wheel spins faster and faster. It can be really hard to find a way to make the wheel stop spinning.

It often seems like the harder you try, the more difficult something becomes. And the more frustrated you get, the more upset you feel.

What is your frustration telling you?

Sometimes your frustration could be telling you that what you're doing isn't working.

At other times, frustration can be a sign that you're almost there, if only you can step back from your frustrated feelings.

When frustration tells you you're close to figuring something out, it might be time to try something a little bit differently.

Or it might be
a message to be calm and
try for just a bit longer.

We've been trying and trying. I feel like we're almost there.

You can't always make things happen exactly the way you want them to. But there are still things you can do! You can learn helpful ways to manage frustration.

Spot the signs of frustration

When did you last feel frustrated about something? How did you feel? What did you do?

Did you feel angry? Did you feel like you wanted to scream at the top of your lungs? Did you feel like you just wanted to give up and not bother trying anymore?

These are warning
signs that your
frustration
is building.

These signs tell
you that you need
to get off the
wheel so you can
stop spinning.

13

Try to calm down

When you spot the signs that frustration
is building, you know you need to calm down.
Here are a few ideas.

Count to four as you breathe in. Then count to four
as you breathe out. Each time you breathe out,
imagine you're blowing out all the frustration
you're feeling. Do this a few times.

You could squeeze a pillow really hard and tell yourself that you're squishing away your frustration.

Or you could run really fast on the spot to get your frustration out.

I feel better now.

Or you might want to just let it all out by crying for a while.

Step back from frustration

If you keep trying to do something and it's just not working, it's a good idea to take a break.

Frustration often happens when you're struggling with something that is difficult to do. It can help you step back and calm down if you turn to something that you find easy or fun, like drawing or reading. Or you might do something more active, like kicking a ball or riding a bike.

Stepping back and taking a break can give you time to calm down, feel better, and think more clearly. Then it will be easier to figure out a more helpful way to deal with the problem.

Break it down

When you've calmed down, you might want to try again. Sometimes breaking down a task into smaller parts can help. Think about how you could do it one bit at a time, rather than trying to get everything right at once.

Alex kept trying to learn a skateboarding trick, but she just couldn't get it right.

She felt herself getting frustrated, so she went inside and played with her dog for a while.

When Alex felt calmer, she decided to try again. She thought about how she could do the trick one step at a time. First she practiced jumping on her board.

Then she practiced flicking the board and jumping at the same time.

Last of all, she made sure she landed back on the board. In the end she put the parts together to do the trick!

Look for a different way

At other times, you might need to
look for a different way to do something.

For his homework, Joel had to make a model rocket. He planned to use an empty plastic bottle, some paper, and some cardboard. He looked in the recycling bin but couldn't find an empty plastic bottle. He looked in the kitchen cupboards, but all the bottles were full.

Joel started to feel frustrated, but when he noticed
his frustration building, he stopped what he was doing.
He took a deep breath. He thought about what he could do
next and decided to look for something else he could use.
He found an empty cardboard tube in the recycling
bin and used that instead of a bottle.

Think of something else to do

Waiting can be frustrating! When you're feeling frustrated because you have to wait, it's helpful to think of something else to do.

Luis and his brother were taking turns playing a game. When Luis realized he was getting impatient and frustrated waiting for his turn, he decided to do something else until his brother had finished.

Devi had been waiting for ten minutes to go on a ride, and was feeling impatient. The line was moving very slowly, and Devi felt super frustrated.
Then she thought, "I know—Dad and I can play 'I Spy' while we wait."

Ask for help

There might be times when you feel frustrated because you don't quite understand how to do something. This can feel even worse when other people seem to do it easily.

But you don't have to feel frustrated and stuck.
You can ask someone to help you!
Explain that you're getting frustrated
and you'd like some help.

Sami was struggling with his homework because he didn't understand the question.

He was getting frustrated. Rather than get angry or give up, he decided to ask someone else for help. He asked his sister Nour.

Let go of frustration

Sometimes you can't make things happen the way you want them to or when you want them to. Perhaps, no matter how hard you try, you just can't do something as well as you'd like. And sometimes you can't change a situation you don't like.

Why can't we go to the movie? Mom said she'd take us last weekend and she didn't, and now we can't again?!

I know, I'm frustrated too. But she got called into work again. How about we go to the park instead?

Rather than get more and more frustrated,
you can try to let go of your frustration.

One way to let go of frustration is to remind yourself
that when there's nothing you can do to change a
situation, there's no point getting mad, sad, or upset.
It won't change things and it won't make things better.

Instead, you can do something else—something you enjoy! This
will help you step back from frustration and feel better.

Step back from frustration

You've learned that you can get frustrated when things don't happen the way you expected. It's like something is in the way of what you want to do or have. You get close, but it's just out of reach. But there's good news: you can learn to manage frustration. Here are some reminders:

- Learn to spot the warning signs of frustration.

- Think about what your frustration is telling you.

- Take a step back and do things that can help you let the frustration out and calm down, like breathe deeply or squeeze a pillow.

- Find a different way to do something. Break it down into small steps.

- Ask someone to help you.

- When you can't change the situation, try to let go of frustration and do something else.

If your frustration feels too big to handle, ask a grown-up for help. If you don't feel you can ask anyone you know, you can call **1-800-448-3000**, text **CONNECT** to **741741**, or go to **yourlifeyourvoice.org** to talk with a counselor. They will listen to you and give you some help and advice about what to do if you're frustrated about something.

Now you know how to tell when you feel frustrated.

And how to step back from your frustration!

Activities

These drawing and writing activities can help you think more about how to manage feeling frustrated. You could keep your pictures and writing with this book so that you have your own ideas about how to cope when you're frustrated by something.

- Look in the mirror and make a frustrated face. Draw a picture of your frustrated face. Then add a thought bubble to your picture with a way to cope with your frustration.

- Think of a time when you felt frustrated. What was it that you couldn't do or that didn't happen? How did you feel? What did you do? Draw a picture or write a story about what happened.

- What are some warning signs that you're getting frustrated? Draw a picture of what happens in your body when you're frustrated.

- Write about or draw a picture of some of the things you could do to turn your mind away from frustration and make room for calmer, more helpful thoughts.

- India is getting frustrated because she just can't get to the next level in her video game. What do you think India could do about it? Write a letter to India with your advice for what she could do next time she's struggling to reach the next level in the game.

- Sometimes when Tom plays with his older brother and sister, they don't listen to his ideas for things they could do together. Tom gets frustrated and upset with them. Then they tease him and he gets even more frustrated and upset. What ideas do you have for Tom? Write down the advice you would give him.

Notes for teachers, parents, and other adults

Whatever triggers their frustration—whether it's unfulfilled needs, unresolved problems, being unable to change something, or not succeeding no matter how hard they try—when children get frustrated they feel powerless. And if they get frustrated too often, they may think that no matter what they do, they won't be able to make something happen or achieve something they want to do.

How you respond to children's frustration will affect how they learn to deal with it. If you get upset with them, their feelings may escalate and quickly turn into anger and despair, further preventing them from managing the source of their frustration. If, though, you respond to children's frustration by asking what the problem is and asking if they need help dealing with it, they will be more likely to calm down and follow your lead in looking for a solution.

Children benefit from effective techniques and strategies to help them feel in control. *Step Back from Frustration* explains ways children can cope when feelings of frustration arise and offers a range of strategies to calm down and gain control of the situation—strategies you can help children with. The book presents suggestions for ways to step back from whatever is frustrating them so children can think more clearly and find a solution, such as breaking a difficult task down into smaller steps or finding a different way to achieve something.

Although children can read this book by themselves, it will be more helpful if you read it together. And while some children might want to read the book all at once, others will find it easier to manage and understand by reading a few pages at a time. Either way, you'll find plenty to talk about together. Talk with children about situations that frustrate them. Talk about the characters in the illustrations. Ask questions such as "Do you ever feel like that?" "What do you think of that idea?" "How could that work for you?"

Taking some time to think about how things have worked out after an episode of frustration helps children learn about themselves and what does and doesn't work for them. Praise children's efforts at this, no matter how small. This will build children's confidence that they have the tools to cope with frustration when it arises. If something a child tried didn't turn out so well, talk together about how things could have gone differently.

After reading the book and helping children identify some strategies that might work for them, you could come back to the book to remind yourselves of the ideas and suggestions for managing frustration.

With patience, support, and encouragement from you, children can learn to cope with and better manage frustrating situations. However, if you're concerned that frustration is frequently overwhelming a child and leading to anger and distress, it's worth seeking more advice. Reach out to a healthcare provider, a counselor, or another expert and ask for help.